MW00942548

Published in the United States of America in 2013 by Gisele Veilleux

CID: 13721073
AID: 13721073
Pages: 137
Publication Date: 2013-03-15 12:57:27.508075-05
ISBN 978-1-300-84022-0
Agency: Bowker

Deaf Dogs Hear with Their Hearts:

An Aussie Named China

By Gisele Veilleux

The Dog Liberator

August 10, 2010

I was working on the computer, updating all of my dogs on the blog and on Petfinder when my phone rang. It was Amber Halsey. She was frantic.

I had rescued a few dogs from the shelter where she worked in Kingsland, Georgia. We talked from time to time about how working with unwanted animals can cause a person to suffer from PTSD and severe depression.

Amber was talking very fast, and I had a hard time understanding her. "They are going to kill her, Gisele. They are going to put her down because she's scared. She is afraid of all of us; she won't let us near her. She sits in the far corner her kennel, and when anyone walks by her she shakes like crazy. She is so scared. They have listed her as a fear biter on her kennel card and if I don't do something by today, now, they are putting her down."

I calmed Amber down a bit, and explained that I needed information before I can help her. I needed basic details, like her age, breed, where she came from, and her overall health.

Amber took a deep breath and tried to answer all of my questions. "The dog is less than a year old, maybe 6 months. She's an Aussie, probably a purebred. She looks very healthy, she's not emaciated, and she has a healthy looking coat. God, Gisele, she is trembling so bad."

I got Amber to focus once again, and asked her to describe the dog's markings.

"Well, she's mostly white, and she has blue eyes."

That's when the entire conversation shifted. "Amber, is she a lethal white?" I asked.

"What does that mean, lethal?" She stuttered.

"Amber, she's scared because she's deaf! She can't hear you coming, she has no where to hide. They call them lethal whites because breeders usually put them down, they can't sell them because they are defective. Most of them are completely deaf and have severe vision issues," I explained.

Amber was quiet for a moment. "You can't take her, can you?" She asked.

"Send me a photo of her. I want to see her eyes. I'll know as soon as you send me a photo," I explained.

I didn't want to give Amber hope, but I didn't want her to give up hope on the dog either.

"Tell them I'm looking at her, and to give me time," I explained.

I sat nervously waiting for Amber to deliver. Within an hour I received these photos taken with a cell phone camera.

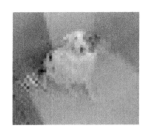

The photos were terribly blurry. The dog was obviously healthy, and very white.

I called Amber and confirmed that the dog was probably completely deaf, and I couldn't tell if she was visually impaired or not. Amber's replied with a simple, "Oh, I understand." She was sure my answer would be no. I then told her that I would take the dog. Amber immediately made notes on the dog's kennel card that the dog was going to rescue, and instantly the dog was safe.

Amber agreed to continue to share information with me about the dog, and she promised to call me later in the evening.

August 11, 2010

Amber shared more information about the dog. It was hard for her to spit it out, but the truth about the little Aussie was crazy.

"I personally know her owner, Gisele. We went to college together. She's a single Mom, recently divorced, and has two young kids. She got the dog as a pup from a breeder, and bought her to breed her.

She told me that the pup was not good with kids, and that the pup bit one of her children."

I found myself in a situation where I had just promised to rescue a dog that had a bite history. This was not good. I didn't want to discriminate against the dog; she's deaf after all.

I asked Amber if the shelter could give the dog a heartworm test, the necessary shots, and spay her.

"There's no way we can do that. You can do a rescue pull without any vetting, but the staff won't get close to her," she regrettably explained.

When a shelter labels a dog as un-adoptable, they will not follow any protocols that they usually follow for adoption. They will, however, execute a rescue pull, which means the dog gets out, without any vetting, at no charge. Basically, they wash their hands of any responsibility.

"Has she shown her teeth or growled at anyone?" I asked her.

"No, but I think she will if we push her," Amber replied.

We discussed the dog's transport. Amber mentioned her friend Donna might be able to help.

Later that day, Amber confirmed that the dog was coming to me on the 14th.
This gave me plenty of time to create a plan for the dog. I didn't know if the dog was dog-aggressive, if she'll bite my kids, or she was a flight risk.

I had a backup plan for everything, but if only dogs could read memos.

I informed my children what we were about ready to do, and my main message was, "Stay away from the dog this time!"

August 14, 2010

I met Donna in my driveway and observed the shy little creature they had named Lilly. She tugged on her collar, wanting to badly to escape, but we managed to get her inside my house.

I had a crate ready for her, but instead of placing it with the other dogs in a separate room; I put it under a desk, and left the crate door open. Lilly spotted the crate immediately and dove in for safety.

I was careful to remove her leash; she was terrified but did not make any advances toward me.

Donna and I sat on the floor talking. I had never personally met Donna before. I was nervous about the dog, wanting to evaluate her, but I was also trying to communicate with Donna to make her feel welcome.

My then eleven year-old son Ryan came home from school. I let him walk toward the crate, and put his hand next to it. Surprisingly, the dog leaned forward and tried to lick his hand. Donna and I stared at each. We expected the dog to growl at my son, not lick him. Ryan was very proud of himself.

A moment later, my then seven year-old daughter Sarah came home from school, and the dog lit up with excitement. She moved herself close to the crate door, and watched every move my daughter made. She wagged her stubby tail, and when Sarah approached her crate, the dog rolled over on her back and exposed her belly.

Of course, one of the first things the kids wanted to know was her name. Her name was too common, Lilly, and we had a rule at The Dog Liberator®, and that is no two dogs should have the same name.

My kids had some ideas; even Donna suggested a few names, but I was hesitant. I hadn't rescued that many Aussies and wasn't that familiar with the breed and its standards, but they appeared to be very similar to the Border Collie. Oh sure, there were a few differences, but the intelligence, the beauty, and the drive was the same.

I looked at the dog carefully and noticed the color of her eyes. When a Border Collie is born merle, they usually have blue eyes, and those eyes are referred to as "china eyes."

I thought about her new name for a moment and continued to watch her trembling from being pathetically insecure. She was delicate and very fragile like china. Her name was chosen.

Donna had a long ride home, so I walked her to her car, and was anxious to release China to see how she would interact with my children.

I promised Donna that I would stay in touch, and keep her updated on China's progress.

When I got back into the house, my daughter's competitive nature kicked into overdrive. My son, Ryan was bragging about how the dog had given him a kiss first (through the crate). That's all Sarah needed to take over and show her brother that the dog loved her more. Oh dear!

I noticed that the dog was not at all nervous when my dogs approached her crate. She actually became somewhat calm with another dog around.
Knowing I couldn't leave her in a crate all day long, I had to start somewhere! I opened the door of the crate slowly and allowed her to exit. She would not. She

sat in the crate nervously staring and shaking.

Everything I had taught my daughter was ignored that day. "No touch, no talk, no eye contact" was our rule. I figured I had two things going for me. Firstly, my daughter was very dog savvy, and wasn't going to put up with any shenanigans from any dog. Secondly, the dog was really interested in her. But still, the dog would not leave the safety of her crate.

I got out of my chair to answer the phone, only traveling a few feet away, and turned my back for a moment while at the same time, Sarah bolted down the hallway to her bedroom. The dog darted from her crate and followed the child.

I quickly followed in pursuit, and when I arrived at Sarah's doorway, China was on Sarah's bed, licking her face. When I entered the room, however, China panicked and ran into Sarah's closet.

Sarah's closet was not the neatest, and that's no place for a dog to be. Sarah's books, toys and clothes plummeted to the floor covering the poor dog.

"If you want the dog to stay in your room, you better clean your closet," I ordered.

I walked away, leaving her bedroom door open, and heard quite a bit of thumping for the next thirty minutes. I turned the television down so I could hear Sarah should something happen. I was cautious but hopeful. The last thing the dog needed was for me to show nervousness, what she did need was for me to show confidence. Since the dog couldn't hear my voice, she'd have to feel my energy.

It was still early in the day, and dinner had to be prepared, chores had to be done, and life must go on.

Every single time I entered Sarah's room, China dove into her closet. It was me she was afraid of. Again, dogs can't read memos, and it was up to me to put the pieces of the puzzle together so I could fully understand the dog's issues, and properly re-home her when the time was right.

China had no trouble with my children, but she was terrified of me. The kennel card said she was not good with children; someone had lied.

I asked Sarah to put a leash on China's collar, and leave it on. It was time for the dogs to eat and go outside to do their business. China dove into Sarah's closet. I grabbed her leash, tugged on it, and walked toward the bedroom door. I needed to take her to the porch and feed her with the other dogs, but she put on the brakes and bucked like a wild horse. It was heartbreaking to see for myself that the dog would rather die of self-inflicted injuries than to go with me. I caved and brought her dinner into Sarah's room.

Several minutes later, again, I pulled her out of the closet to take her outside. It was a no go. Sarah took her leash, and while the dog didn't fight as much, she would not go through the doorway and walk pass me. I literally had to leave the room. Sarah walked the dog outside, and there were no issues.

Ryan joined us outside, and I had my camera. I sat in the middle of the yard hoping China would walk pass me. She did well with my dogs, Ozzie and Lady Di.

I came up with several scenarios that might explain her behavior, but was too appalled to believe that I was right.

Later that night, I downloaded the photos from my camera onto my computer and analyzed them.

When I zoomed into the photo of her in the crate, I noticed something wrong with her eyes. One of her pupils was not centered. I was more convinced that she was completely deaf, because I had reason to believe she was also visually impaired.

I also reviewed the photos with her and Ryan, and I noticed her body language. While at first she was sure of herself when Ryan wasn't paying attention to her, she cowered and was unsure of him when he made eye contact with her.

No Concern

Afraid

Unsure but curious

Still Cautious

More Relaxed

Both Sarah and Ryan freely accepted her into the family, and so did the pack. I was going to have to trust this dog and allow my children to help her trust adults, especially adult women.

I knew she had bitten or tried to bite a child in her former home, so while I had to give her a chance, I had to be cautious. I reminded the kids several times a day to be careful with her. Still, I knew I was talking out of both sides of my mouth.

This wouldn't be the first time an owner who surrendered their dog to the pound completely misrepresented the dog.

I remembered one dog that I rescued years ago, his name was Jet. I saw on Jet's paperwork that he was absolutely not good with kids. Moments after he entered my back yard, my fearless daughter wanted to meet him. I busted out laughing.

August 15, 2010

The kids were at school, and China was sleeping in Sarah's closet again. I was expecting a volunteer foster to come over to deliver some paperwork. Nancy came into the house, but before I'd let her leave, I wanted her to see what I saw.

She followed me into Sarah's bedroom and saw the pup in her closet sleeping.

I lay flat on the floor and took a long back scratcher and reached toward China, eventually tapping her foot. Startled, she jumped and backed up into the closet, hugging the back wall. She trembled so profusely I thought all of her hair would fall out.

Nancy couldn't believe it. She too had never seen such a pitiful sight. "How long have you had her?" She asked.

"Only 24 hours," I explained. "She stays here all day until my daughter comes home. Once my daughter is home, she follows her around. She's great, as long as she doesn't see me."

"She has been beaten by a woman," Nancy said matter-of-factly.

I agreed with Nancy. I suspected it, but hearing it from someone else made it real. I didn't want to believe that someone would beat this dog. Sadly, I strongly believed she was abused because they didn't know she was deaf. But how deaf was she?

Later that afternoon, I picked up the kids from school and stopped Sarah from going into her room. I slammed the door hard, rang the door bell, and we grabbed pots and pans making all the noise we could as we walked down the hallway toward Sarah's bedroom.

When we entered her room, China was sleeping soundly. We stopped making noise and heard her snoring faintly. It was adorable, but it was sad at the same time.

August 17, 2010

I know that it takes time for a dog to improve especially the shy fearful dogs, but I was getting frustrated with China. She used my children like body guards, as if I was going to hurt her. It was time for me to step up to the plate and kick this up a notch!

This time, when Sarah left for school, she closed her bedroom door behind her. China would have to find a place to hide, and all she had was a crate; the same crate she visited on her first day. The crate was under a desk, which was right next to my desk.

I returned from dropping the kids off, and China had hunkered down in the crate.

I left the crate door open, and went about my business. Each time I left the room, I noticed a new article in her crate.

Throughout the day, China was waiting for me to leave, either to get coffee or use the restroom, and she would slink off into the bathroom to retrieve an article of dirty clothes from the hamper that belonged to Sarah.

Eventually, I even saw a hair brush in her crate. I knew she was jumping up on the vanity to steal the things that she wanted to make her den complete. China was a collector!

It was then that I drew upon my memories of Nutella. Early in 2010, I rescued a tiny little thing from Chilton County Humane Society in Alabama. She too was labeled a fear biter. The shelter had named her Lassie. She may have been a year old. I never saw very much puppy behavior in her, so maybe she was older. Even her shelter photo looked intimidating!

While I clearly saw her hair standing up on her back, her tail between her legs, her eyes looking forward at the person who was scaring her, and her teeth showing, I could hear her deliver a low warning growl in the photo!

Her second shelter photo wasn't as frightening.

Because she was tiny, I figured I'd give her a try, not realizing what I was getting myself into.

I renamed her Nutella. For the first two days, she viciously showed her teeth anytime I opened her crate. I had to carry her in the crate outside, and open the door for her to relieve herself. This routine got really old really fast!

She darted around the yard, going in the opposite direction of wherever I was. She wanted absolutely no contact.

At first glance, she was feral, but I talked myself out of that rational quickly, when I suspected she was just scared to death; but why? What had someone done to this little creature that made her so frightened?

After two days of this unnatural behavior, I had had enough; I couldn't live this way anymore. Something had to give.

I brought her crate, with her in it, into the house and set it down by the entrance way of my home. My dogs approached her, and she perked up quickly. Once she had begun to wag her tail and show interest, I bravely opened her crate door. She was now in my house!

Her anxiety immediately improved just by being next to my dogs. Suddenly, something set her back to that place of fear and she flew under my desk – perfect!

I had a large quilt ready for her. I cornered her under my desk and bagged her with the quilt. Wrapping it all around her, she had nowhere to go.

I sat in a large comfortable chair and held her, slowly peeling back the comforter so that I could only see her little face. Her eyes bulged out in horror; she thought I was going to kill her.

Holding her tight, I did not engage in eye contact. I quietly talked to myself, talking about my day and what I had left to do. I pretended I was talking to a friend in the room, not to her!

After about five minutes had passed, she began to relax. I slowly placed my fingers on top of her head and began to lightly scratch her ears. The more she relaxed, I began to talk to her directly, and occasionally glanced down at her.

She was enjoying the warmth of the blanket, the softness of my voice, the comfort of my grip, and the pleasure of her ears being rubbed. After five more minutes, she fell asleep.

I let her have a little nap until a volunteer came over and we decided that the pup needed a bath. She had been relieving herself in her crate, and she smelled! She went straight into the shower, and believe it or not, she did very well! After her shower, she was bundled again in a large towel and went right back into that chair, and then fell asleep in my volunteer's arms for at least an hour! It was over!

I continued Nutella's rehabilitation and tied her leash to my waist so that she went everywhere with me. When it was time for bed, I wrapped her leash around my arm and we slept together. This quickly became a habit! It wasn't long before I would find her on my pillow after 8:00 PM every night, waiting for me.

After one week, I was able to take her to the front yard, and this photo was taken. She did not try to run away for she was not afraid. She relaxed in my arms, enjoying the sunlight on her face and getting kisses!

She also enjoyed sitting in my lap and hanging onto me like a monkey while I worked on my computer!

Of course, I posted her progress and her photos of transformation on Facebook. It was amazing!

Nutella was adopted. Even during her meet with her new family she acted terrified. They had plenty of experience dealing with quirky little dogs.

Even though she did not show affection and avoided them, they wanted to bring her home. I was reluctant at first, thinking that they should come to my house several times and get to know her before they bring her home, but they won!

My Nutty Buddy went home with them, and settled in quickly. Today, she is the diva she was always meant to be. She is adored, and I still miss her!

Ashley and Nutella, who is now called Zelda

Because I had Nutella under my belt, I drew upon my experiences, found my inner strength, and tried to remain calm, knowing that somehow China was going to have to get over it.

August 20, 2010

In an effort to increase China's exposure on social media outlets, I asked photographer Olivia Frost to do a photo shoot with China and me. If you notice, I'm holding onto her and her leash! Oh sure, she might look happy, but she'd really rather bolt and hide! At least she allowed me to touch her!

I posted the photos, and while I heard rave reviews of how gorgeous she was, I still wasn't getting emails from interested adopters.

After I posted these photos on Facebook, a few people were hinting that I should keep her. "Keep" is not an option in rescue! Notice the leash?

After seeing the photos on Facebook, Amber called me. She was thrilled with China's progress. I knew that it would take a while for me to find China the perfect home. I was prepared to keep her until that perfect family was found. I assured Amber that China's new home would be her forever home.

August 21, 2010

I had purposely made steak for dinner, and I made extra this time. I let the dogs hover around the dining room table, and we took turns handing out little steak bites.

With her legs outstretched, prepared to make a quick getaway, China cautiously accepted the steak bites from us, using our dogs as a shield of course. When I felt her lips against my fingers, it was kind of nice to know she was getting closer.

I watched her follow Sarah around all night long. Running back and forth from her room to the living room while I helped Sarah with homework, China was her shadow.

This dog has captured my heart, hook, line, and sinker, and I thank God that she came to us.

August 28, 2010

China was still fearful of adults. She wanted to trust, but she couldn't. She was stuck; frozen in fear. She didn't know how to let go of the past, and because of that, she was missing out on a lot.

I wasn't convinced that her former owner beat her severely, after speaking with behaviorist Paul Pipitone; he explained that some dogs are so sensitive it only takes one slap to send them into panic-stricken fear. "When we see a dog's behavior and believe it's been beaten," he explained, "It doesn't mean it really was beaten. Some dogs are so highly intelligent and sensitive that all it takes is one swat with a newspaper, and you're done; the dog will no longer trust you."

Maybe they beat her; maybe they didn't.
Maybe they just scared her to death,
snuck up on her, and kept her in a
constant state of fear. I knew that China
was suffering emotionally, and I couldn't
bear to watch it any longer. I had given
her more time than I gave Nutella; giving
her any more time was not going to help.

There's a time to be patient with a dog,
and there's a time to just get on with it.

I tucked Sarah in for the night and told
her that I was taking China. Sarah was
not happy, but I asked her to trust me.

I know that dogs can't read or write
memos, but if they could, here's what
China was thinking that night:

"*Uh oh, she's putting a leash on me. Here comes the gentle tug, but I'd rather stay in my crate. Oh well, okay, I'll follow you, but where are we going?*

In your bedroom? No, no, no, you don't understand, I only sleep with children, I don't like adults. I am not comfortable here, and I don't want to be next to you.

Where's my girl?

What? You want me to jump in bed with you? Well... I feel that tug on the leash, but I'm terrified of you, and I don't know this bed. You're going to have to pull harder than that, I do not want to comply. Okay, I'll jump up, but I'm not getting too close.

Okay, I'm up, you can pet me now but in a few minutes, I'm out of here.

Okay, I'm leaving now. Woops, I feel that tug again. I guess I'll have to stay for a minute or two.

Where's my girl?

Ahhhh, I love having my ears rubbed, let me get a little closer. Kiss my nose? Are you crazy lady, that's way too close for me. Well, okay, just this one time.

Let me accidentally roll over on my back so you can rub my belly. Wow! You have finger nails and they really feel good. Okay, I guess I can kiss you back. This is really fun, and it doesn't hurt, but I have to leave now. I'm not supposed to be here, and I'm not supposed to be with you."

China rolled over and fell asleep, pressing her back against mine, and maintained close contact with me until about 4:00 AM, when she tried to jump off the bed again. I held the leash, which was wrapped around my arm, and she settled back down at my feet.

At 5:00 AM, I decided she had done well, and I opened my bedroom door. I rewarded her by allowing her to bolt into Sarah's room. She jumped up on Sarah's bed, curled into a ball, and stared at me as I left.

We continued this game of trust and our progress was swift. We must be pack leaders with our dogs if we want them to feel safe. Even though she knew I would never hurt her, she just couldn't let go and trust me. Now she knew that nothing had happened to her, and she had survived.

Over the following days, China had amassed quite a collection of stolen items in her crate. It started with Sarah's t-shirt and then a sock, but later she found a rather large wicker basket and squeezed it into her crate. She has collected balls, blankets, towels, brushes and dog toys. While there is nothing unusual about this, what is unusual is that I never caught her doing it. For a deaf dog, she knew how to get around undetected.

Ryan has been taking her outside and throwing the tennis ball for her. She loved it. She made crazy sounds when

she catches them in mid-air. She
sounded like a moose in distress, much
like Chewbacca of Star Wars. The kids
call her Chibacca. I guess deaf dogs can't
hear how ridiculous they sound.

August 21, 2010

A month passed, and life went on at The Dog Liberator. I was fostering several dogs, using my pack to socialize them, and facilitating their adoptions. China was quite a foster. She played with the new dogs and had wonderful manners.

During adoptions, I sometimes let the pack out, including China, to allow her to meet strangers. It never failed that she was terrified of strangers, especially women.

I provided visitors with treats, asking them to invite her to take one. Sometimes she did; sometimes she didn't.

During the day while I worked, she had learned that when I opened the refrigerator door, she would get a hot dog bite. She was starting to get closer to me and less fearful.

One day, while Sarah was in the bathtub, I was in bed suffering from a cold, and China snuck into my room and peeked up at me. I tapped on my bed, and much to my surprise, she jumped up and cuddled with me, for only a minute, before something told her to be afraid, and once again, she bolted.

China fit in very well with Ozzie and Lady Di. She continued to do well with new foster dogs as well. They took turns playing with each other, but more importantly, China was very submissive with Lady Di, which is necessary to survive here!

Ryan took these photos one afternoon, I was very impressed! They were later used on our 2011 calendar!

The photo gave me a glimpse of my future and represented the three breeds that I would focus on throughout my efforts in rescue; the border collie, rough collie, and the Australian shepherd.

September 8, 2010

China's behavior continued to improve. She was beginning to socialize with strangers. Emily, one of my volunteers, came over often, and tried to gain China's trust.

She was getting closer and closer to strangers during adoptions. But no one was interested in adopting her yet. She was still too scared. Most potential adopters felt that China would not be a good watch dog; being deaf, she would fail to bark. I couldn't convince them otherwise.

One evening Sarah was listening to music in her room. She had her MP3 player and was wearing her head phones. While sitting in a computer chair, she began to spin, and sing to herself, closing her eyes and enjoying her quiet time.

Without warning, China bit her in the belly. I heard a horrendous scream, and Sarah ran out of her room, crying.

I couldn't understand what she was saying. Clearly, the dog had bitten her, but why. Sarah repeated what happened, but it didn't make any sense to me.

The mark was large, but the dog had not broken the skin, though the bruising was severe. To the right of Sarah's belly button, China had left a mark larger than a silver dollar.

Sarah panicked, of course, realizing what an unprovoked bite means in rescue: it's not good.

I shared the incident with several fellow rescuers, and they all urged me to get rid of the dog as soon as possible. One of my dearest friends warned me that it would happen again; next time it would be worse and I would have no choice but to give her up. A rescuer does not surrender a rescued dog.

Sarah understood the gravity of China's actions. I could I not let Sarah down, and I couldn't let China down either.

Later that evening, we re-created the situation.

"You just want me to spin again Mommy?" She asked. "Yes dear, spin, just like you were before she bit you."

I watched China look at Sarah, and look away; look at Sarah, look away. China was nervous. She was concerned, she was confused. She didn't know what to do. What I witnessed was a dog that saw its human, the human it loved more than any other human, spinning out of control. The human's eyes were closed, the human's head was back, and it looked odd. No, it looked more than odd; it looked as if the human was in pain. Something was very wrong with the human. Humans do not spin like that, humans do not move that way. This human is in trouble.

As I continued to observe, everything about China's body language changed. She panicked. She must rescue her human. Her human needs help, her human must stop. Her human is hurt.

China's eyes got wide, and she positioned herself in a way that I knew she was getting read to lunge at Sarah.

With tremendous confidence and authority I quickly stood between her and Sarah, and pointed at her. Walking into her, I forced China to step away and back off. China got it! She jumped up on Sarah's bed and I froze, pointing at her, not letting her escape me. I made myself very clear to the dog.

"This is not your job. Children spin!"

China thought she was in trouble, but now was not the time to punish her. I believe that China thought I was going to hit her. Hitting her was not an option; hitting her would not achieve the results that I wanted. With my body language and my energy, I told China to "leave it, this [the child] doesn't belong to you, this belongs to me, and I'm in charge."

I waited until China submitted to me. She relaxed her body, lowered her head, and lay completely flat on the bed, rolling over on her back, exposing her belly, and we were done.

I told Sarah we were finished now.
"That's it? We're done? What happened?" She asked.

"From now on, when you spin, I want you to do it in the living room in front of me, but I don't think we'll have a problem again," I explained.

"Did you spank her, Mommy?" She asked.

"No, we never have to spank dogs.
Spanking doesn't teach them anything but
to be afraid of you," I explained.

For some reason, I felt confident that the
issue would never repeat itself. I felt that
I had communicated with China, and we
had an understanding. I'm the Mom; you
are the dog!

That night, after Sarah fell asleep I found
a note that she had written. She was
expressing her love and compassion for
the dog, and how bad she wanted to keep
her. Even after she had been bit by
China, she still wanted to keep her.

October 16, 2010

Just a short month prior to our annual reunion, I had mentioned to a few of my friends that I hoped China would be ready for a public outing. They shunned the idea, telling me I would traumatize her. HA!

Our first annual reunion was on, and I invited both Amber and Donna to come and see China again. Amazing isn't it?

Amber, China and Donna

Several people who had been to my house earlier couldn't believe she was the same dog. China walked from person to person, sniffing, and getting pets. She was not afraid, she had her pack, and she had her human, Sarah.

Notice the slack on the leash. China literally follows Sarah everywhere!

Photographer, Olivia Frost sapped a photo of my new pack, it was breathtaking!

November 6, 2010

With the reunion behind us, and it was time for a short break. We went home and enjoyed a break from rescue and the next few weeks were very uneventful. China continued to improve with strangers. Sarah would sleep with me on occasion, and China would join us. She wasn't afraid of me as much.

Friends who would visit frequently began to expect a pleasant greeting from China, but she was still stealing things throughout the house!

I noticed a lot about China. She had this internal 2 minute rule when she was outside. Every two minutes, she would look for me. Did she do this out of fear? Was she wondering where I was, wanting to be sure where I was? Was she afraid that I would sneak up on her? This internal clock made it easy to train her.

When I called my dogs to come inside, they would ignore me. Ozzie will continue stalking squirrels and Lady Di would continue to sun herself, but China would see me and come inside.

How can I explain to the public that only the deaf dog listens to me?

China's internal clock also made it easy for me to correct her. When I caught her digging a hole, all I had to do was wait for the 2 minutes to pass. She would look up at me, I'd point my finger and shake my head, and she would slink low to the ground in shame and abandon her hole, even though I never spoke a word.

I began to realize that if I communicated with my dogs by only using my body language without trying to talk to them, I would be more successful; and I was.

China was also more expressive than other dogs. She ran in circles when we came home from an outing, but she never jumped on us. Yes, she was excited, but she was not rude.

I noticed that all I had to do to invite her was to make eye contact with her and nod my head. The level of control that I had over her was amazing, and it was easy.

I began to brag about how easy it was to train her. After one try, she had sit, stay, shake and lay down; all with hand signals.

When I brought her to the vet for her shots, the technicians surrounded her in the examination room. They asked me how I tell her "good girl."

"Just wiggle your body!" I laughed. It was hard to explain, so I had to show them. Just shake your head and wiggle your body, that's what she does when she's happy, so we do it back. It's our way of inviting her to play. Sure enough, one slight wiggle and she lit up with joy!

November 9, 2010

One of my rescued dogs, Gemini, was being adopted by a young boy, and he had read so much about Sarah and China that he wanted to meet them! They drove from Clearwater, Florida to my home, and the two youngsters exchanged stories about their dogs. Of course, all during their conversation, I snapped photos like crazy! After all, these were future little Liberators!

What I noticed in the photos is how Sarah carried herself that day. She had pride and confidence. I also saw China's devotion to her.

I wasn't starting to cave at that point, I was just being observant!

November 29, 2010

For months I had painted a picture of what China's home would be like. I imagined a family, with a stay-at-home mom, maybe a few kids (not too many) a great pack of dogs, and family that could continue her behavior modification and increase her self-esteem. China was a work in progress.

I had received several emails from interested adopters, but none of them screamed China. Instead, many of them adopted other dogs from me, and that wasn't a bad thing!

It had been over three months since China came to my home. It didn't take long before Sarah asked me if we could keep her. The answer was always, "No, we can't keep her, but she will be adopted."

Every single night, I'd put Sarah to bed, and she'd ask me, "Mommy, can we keep China?" I don't know where I got my strength from, because the kid should've worn me thin, but I didn't cave. We rescue; we do not keep.

Every night we played the same game. I would ask Sarah, "What do we do when we're in rescue?" She'd cross her arms, turn her head away from me, and pout.

I'd hold up one finger and say, "we rescue..."

Then I'd hold up another finger and say, "we rehabilitate...."

Then I'd hold up another finger and say, "we fully vet..."

Holding the fourth finger, I'd say, "we spay/neuter, and?"

Sarah would scream, "Keep!"

"No Sarah, we do not keep. We re-home."

The same exact conversation would repeat itself every morning on the way to school. "Can we keep her?"

I had two dogs, Ozzie and Lady Di, and I was not going to have three dogs. I not only can't handle the work, but I can't afford it either.

That night, once again, I pictured China's new home and I realized that I was wasting my time. No one had come for China. The emails weren't a fit for her. I knew that I wasn't holding her back. I wasn't sabotaging her adoption. I wasn't being overly picky. I just knew what she needed, and I hadn't found it. I reviewed her photos in an attempt to update her page, and I saw her family.

I went online to my Petfinder and Rescue Groups account, and took her down; I marked her as adopted. I also marked her as adopted on my blog. No one noticed, not even my closest friends. I didn't tell Sarah, and I hoped that she wouldn't notice either. I figured it was another month before Christmas, and whatever happened between now and then was meant to be. I would no longer actively pursue a home for China.

China appeared to use Ozzie as her compass, not wanting to move into new situations without him, and using Sarah as her security blanket. Many times China and Lady Di would team up together to play. It truly was a lovely match.

December 3, 2010

Two young female Aussies were being bounced around on Craig's list, and we knew, based on the description that one of them was probably a lethal white (also referred to as double merle). When I called the people who had put her up on Craig's list, I could hear a dog barking in the background. Then, I knew the dog was deaf! The man denied it, but I wasn't playing around. I asked him to give me the dog. I named her Asia, but the name didn't stick. She was much too pretty, so we renamed her Kiss. Her sister, Sparrow, suffered from a broken leg, an old injury; how does one break a puppy's leg, I ask?

The way little Kiss velcroed herself to China was amazing.

I still don't understand how a white Aussie knows it's a white Aussie. I don't understand why all of the deaf dogs team up with China immediately. Maybe there's a code that we don't know about. Regardless, it happens!

I knew that China was going help me continue to rescue deaf/blind Aussies, as long as they continued to find their way into my rescue.

Kiss was an absolutely stunning dog. She
didn't have the issues that China had.
She was not afraid; as a matter of fact
she was quite dominant and was very
rough with her sister, Sparrow. I also
learned that the deaf dogs can't hear their
siblings yip or growl. So they just keep on
playing hard. It's very easy for a deaf pup
to become the dominant one. Sparrow

was adopted quickly, so I had more time
to spend with Kiss, teaching her manners!

Sarah had fun playing dress up with Kiss,
and Kiss received a lot of socialization
skills because of Sarah. Kiss was later
adopted by a family who had two young
children! I wonder sometimes if they are
still playing dress up with the pup!

December 21, 2010

I found drawings of China all over Sarah's room, as well as notes she had written. Christmas was only a few days away!

Dear Santa,

I know I'm not supposed to ask for this, but I really want my Mom to let us keep my dog China. She is so sweet, and she loves me so much. I know if she gets adopted, she'll miss me and die.

I don't know what you can do to help me get the only thing I want for Christmas this year, but it's a rescued dog. She doesn't see good, and she's really deaf, but she's still a great dog. Thank you.

Love,

Sarah

December 25, 2010

On Christmas morning, after all the presents were opened, I told Sarah that China was hers to keep. Sarah didn't believe me at first, and questioned me, but I assured her that China was NOT available for adoption any longer.

I posted it on Facebook:

China got a bag of tennis balls for Christmas, but the last gift of the morning was Sarah's... it's China. "you mean we can keep her?"
Like · · Share 44 people like this.

Holly R: The best Christmas ever!
December 25, 2010 at 8:00am · Like · 2

Kenia M: I'm sure That's the best gift ever!!!!!!
December 25, 2010 at 8:23am via mobile ·
Like · 2

Kim S-D: I'm crying:) Tears of happiness.
Merry Christmas and God bless.
December 25, 2010 at 8:33am · Like · 3

Jesse M: Sorry Ms. Streep, the award goes to Sarah this year.
December 25, 2010 at 8:33am · Like · 5

Kim S-D: No Gisele, you gave your daughter the gift of pure love:)
December 25, 2010 at 8:34am · Like · 4

The DogLiberator: she looked at me and said... China? You mean, we're keeping her? poor kid, she's been asking me for months... DAILY!!!! My answer has always been, "we'll see".
December 25, 2010 at 8:59am · Like · 2

Julia B: what a great mom you are!
December 25, 2010 at 8:59am · Like · 4

Sarah B: Yey Congrats to all. The waiting might have been hard but sometimes that makes the end of waiting that much more golden!
December 25, 2010 at 9:07am · Like · 3

Amie B: What a perfect gift for China...a family that already knows they love her no matter what
December 25, 2010 at 9:25am · Like · 4

Pam R: awwww Gisele....now that really makes a great Christmas DAY!!!! It tops and trumps my gift .. A WHITE CHRISTMAS in ALABAMA!!!!! Thank you God for all you have done in our lives!!!!! China gets the best gift of all though...her own little "gisele". Merry Christmas to all DOG LIBERATORS...I think I hear Angels singing..oops nope that's CHINA!!!!!
December 25, 2010 at 9:41am · Like · 4

Donna Grunewald: I am so happy for all of you! China gets to stay in the perfect home and now Sarah doesn't have to plan her escape with her! Whenever my Mom says "we'll see" that always meant yes. Merry Christmas!
December 25, 2010 at 9:48am · Like · 3

The DogLiberator: Donna, I'll remember that!!!!!
December 25, 2010 at 10:33am · Like · 2

Anja S-P: Ok, I'm getting off this computer! I keep crying!!!!!
Merry Christmas China!!!! Gisele, you are awesome!!! You must be so proud of Sarah, she has such a precious heart!!!
December 25, 2010 at 11:25am · Like · 3

April McG: How nice Anja - I'm crying too What a wonderful Christmas for all.... China and family!!
December 25, 2010 at 11:40am · Like · 3

Amie B: Now you and Sarah have another thing you can do together. Learn sign to speak with China and all of the other lethal whites you meet in the years to come.....
December 25, 2010 at 11:50am · Like · 2

The DogLiberator: I hope to allow China to serve as a mentor for all double merles i.e., deaf/blind aussies, for years to come.
December 25, 2010 at 1:57pm · Like · 2

Karen L-G: THAT IS SO FREAKING AWESOME!!!!!!!!!!!!!
December 25, 2010 at 1:59pm · Like · 3

Pam R: I'm still hearing the Hallelujah chorus in the background!!!!
December 25, 2010 at 5:05pm · Like · 2

Terry W: Cool !! December 25, 2010 at 10:06pm · Like · 1

Terry Watts Gisele I am so happy for all of you!!! The bestest Christmas Present in the world!! God Bless.
December 26, 2010 at 2:07am · Like · 2

Beckee VanW: YAAAAA!!
December 26, 2010 at 6:12am · Like · 2

February 12, 2011

Today was a day I really looked forward to. A rescuer in Alabama scooped up this pretty ball of white fluff, and she was coming to my house! She was an identical copy of China.

It was amazing how once again, a white Aussie pup, totally deaf, attached herself to China. China took the pup into her heart and began to socialize her immediately. We named her Baby Ga Ga.

She was stunning. I imagined that China must have looked exactly like her.

Sarah was turning eight years-old soon, and her love for dogs grew even stronger. When she met Baby Ga Ga, she was in heaven; we all were. What a cute little thing, and very smart. I thought Sarah would gravitate toward the pup, and ignore China a bit. I waited for her to use the "keep" word again, but it never happened.

I really expected any child to choose a puppy over an adult dog, but it didn't happen.

I now had the proof that nothing could separate Sarah from China.

In rescue, we are tempted by the dogs we foster. We know we can't keep them all, so we have to be very careful when we make the commitment to keep a dog that we have pulled.

When my border collie, Ozzie, came to me, he was given to me by his former owners. I was not actively in rescue at that time. My border collie, Reckless, had recently passed away, and when Ozzie entered my home, he was a fit.

I didn't know at that time that within a few months, my rescue efforts would explode, and I would be in the thick of it all.

I rescued a gorgeous border collie named Tim Tebow whom I would have easily kept. Later the next year, I rescued a dog named Jake, whom I also fell in love with. Just a few months ago, I rescued another wonderful boy named Ziggy. So you see, when I decided to keep Ozzie, the word keep means forever.

If those of us in rescue don't make that commitment seriously, then we are just like everyone else; going through dogs like disposable pens. Keep means keep; and Sarah had proved to me that keep means keep!

Baby Ga Ga was quickly adopted by a former adopter, but not before she spent some time with us and learned the ropes!

I do get updated photos of Baby Ga Ga and she does look exactly like China; it's amazing, and she is also deaf.

November 5, 2011

I bet you think this story is over, but it's not. It took months before Sarah stopped asking me if she's really ours to keep. She would rephrase the question, trying to trip me up; just to be sure that China was staying.

During our 2011 annual reunion, Sarah and China had quite an impressive photo shoot by Olivia Frost. I continued to write about China and her interactions with our foster dogs, especially the deaf/blind ones.

Sarah continues to tell everyone how
perfect and beautiful China is so she
doesn't miss an opportunity to have their
photograph taken together. Even after a
year, the newness had not worn off.

While Sarah loves all of our dogs as well as our foster dogs, China is and will always be her heart dog.

One of the most common criticisms I received when trying to re-home China was that people didn't think she would protect the house, i.e. she wouldn't bark. This is so far from the truth.

When Ozzie and Lady Di hear us coming home, they recognize the sound of the car engine, the sound of the car door slam, and they have the advantage to hear our voices as we enter. While they may stand up anticipating our arrival, they do not bark. China does. China does not have the advantage to know who is coming, she just knows someone is.

What is sad, however, is even if I'm only a few feet from my front door China does not recognize me through the glass. Her vision is so poor, that she must smell me before she stops barking at the alleged stranger.

A drastic change in clothing, for example, will cause a reaction. When familiar children came to my house wearing Halloween costumes, China ducked under my desk and trembled in fear. Costumes were quickly removed for her benefit. Once she recognized the child, she was fine.

You can almost see it in her facial expression once she recognizes you. Her entire energy changes, as if she says, "Oh, I know you!"

One day I exited my room wearing a yellow dress and makeup. China was convinced that a stranger was in the house. She barked at me ferociously and wouldn't come near me. Sarah had to hold onto China's collar, slide her near me so she could smell my hand. China was amazed and relieved that I was Mommy!

November 12, 2011

During Caylee's adoption, photographer
Jessica Savidge was fascinated with China
and took this photo.

China's fear of women is still there, but
when given the time, she will warm up to
many strangers.

Photo by Jessica Savidge

Deaf/Blind Dogs Rescued by TDL

The list grows, because I won't hesitate to take one of these gorgeous dogs if I can, but here is our current list of hearing and/or visually impaired dogs we have rescued to date:

Baileys
Jalo
Diva
Knish
Falcor
Irwin
Dundee
Fiona
Baby Ga Ga
Kiss
Velveteen
Sassafras
Skate

Regardless of the dog's issues, China is a gracious host to our foster dogs, and many who come to visit me ask to meet her. More importantly, many who have grown to love her from a platform called Facebook and want a dog just like her.

As a matter of fact, the Wilson family has adopted several of our deaf dogs, and they have fostered many! To date, they have adopted Irwin, Dundee, and Fiona. As I write this book, they are on their way to evaluate a deaf Aussie boy at Polk County Animal Control, so the list continues to grow!
Here's a photo of Kierstin and Fiona.

December 8, 2012

During our third annual reunion, I heard even more people asking me where they could find a dog like China. It appears she has her own following!

This year, we had the pleasure of having Brittney's Myers as our photographer, and of course, Sarah made sure that her heart dog would be in our photo album!

Sarah created a Facebook for China, as if she's a real person.

Sarah is nine years-old now. Nothing has changed between China and Sarah since she came to our home. She continues to steal things, and she and Sarah are closer than ever. I don't think there's a day that goes by where Sarah doesn't profess her love for the dog.

Out of nowhere, Sarah will squeal, "Isn't she so beautiful?" It's as if China just arrived.

"Of course she's beautiful," I answer her. "She's just as beautiful as she was last week, last month and last year... nothing has changed Sarah; she's beautiful!"

January 26, 2013

The true test of successful rehabilitation can only be live and in real-time. We wanted to be in a parade in downtown DeLand, and I wanted all of my dogs to participate, including China.

Sarah and her classmate Danielle were excited. We bought some bling for the occasion and decided that China would wear pink sequins! She was stunning.

China kept her eyes on us the entire time, but every once and a while, she'd notice we were several feet away and she'd race to catch up to us, but not one person knew she was deaf or visually impaired.

Today, China has taught me so much, I really should thank her! I will not hesitate to rescue a deaf and/or blind dog Aussie. I find them easier to train and more enjoyable to foster!

February 1, 2013

Last November I received a message via Facebook about a stray Aussie in Seminole County that a good Samaritan was trying to catch. Ironically he was eventually caught by animal control in late January. He was identified as being deaf and possibly visually impaired. I had the room and the desire to take him in, so he came to my rescue.

His story is a remarkable one, but in short, we named him Winter. He had emotionally shut down, and was also terrified of humans.

Because I didn't take my time like I did with China, his rehabilitation was immediate. He was adopted one week later by Dale Johnson. Winter is phenomenal. He quickly developed an internal clock and knows exactly what time Dale comes home from work everyday. He sits at the gate, even in the pouring rain at 2:00 PM sharp.

I receive regular updates from Dale, and Winter truly is remarkable.

When I first heard about deaf Aussies in 2009, I couldn't understand why people who had one would go through the trouble to find another. Most of the time, when someone adopts a deaf dog, they do so unknowingly. A breeder sells the dog withholding the information, or the seller, pound, or rescue simply does not know.

Winter with Dale

This begs the question, if you weren't aware that you were bringing home a deaf dog, why would you want another one?

I know the answer to that question. They are truly amazing. They are animated, more devoted, they communicate more, share more, appreciate more, and I hate to say it, but they are more intelligent! No offense to my other two dogs, Ozzie and Lady Di, but deaf dogs rule!

Our first deaf rescue dog was an Old English Sheepdog named Sassafras. She was adopted by a woman named Fritzi in Connecticut. I had many wonderful conversations with Fritzi, and she shared a lot of information that helped me. One evening, Frizi shared with me stories of her deaf OES who had passed away.

She wanted her to compete in agility, but the rules strictly prohibit deaf dogs from entering the competition.

"I won't drink the Kool aid, Gisele. I entered her into Agility anyway, and I never told anyone that she was deaf. She did very well, won many times, and to this day very few people know that she was deaf," Fritzi explained.

Written by Donna Grunewald

I first met China (Lilly at the time) when I was asked by Amber Halsey of the Camden County Humane Society to transport her to The Dog Liberator.

Amber told me that she had been surrendered by the owner who said that she was a biter and not good with children.

Amber saw something different in her and knew what would become of her if she didn't get her to TDL.

I was nervous since this was my first transport, but when I saw this beautiful yet shy dog I was glad that I was taking her somewhere where she would get the chance for a better life.

She was very quiet and well behaved during the three hour ride and finally even took a treat out of my hand. Once we arrived at Gisele's house, I was amazed that Gisele recognized immediately that China was deaf and possibly at least partially blind. No wonder she hadn't been bothered by my singing!

For a dog that had been labeled bad with children she seemed more comfortable with Gisele's children Sarah and Ryan that with Gisele and I. I hated to leave her but I knew that she was in great hands.

After that experience I started following TDL and China's progress via Facebook. I loved seeing the videos of her playing joyfully with Gisele's pack and reading her updates. I especially loved reading about the incredible bond between China and Sarah.

Although I had spent only a few hours with China, I felt such an attachment to her and just hoped that the perfect family would find her.

When I read that Gisele was giving China to Sarah for Christmas I was ecstatic. She had been with the perfect family all along!

When Gisele announced the TDL reunion both Amber and I knew that we had to go.

Seeing China there was like seeing a completely different dog. She followed Sarah everywhere with her head high. She was the queen of the ball! Her fearfulness and shyness was gone, replaced by a happy, playful and joyous dog that was not held back by her deafness and partial blindness. It was so great to be able to hug her at last!

Amber, China and Donna

Lethal Whites

For more information about the term "Lethal White" visit the White Aussies Project Website, but understand that many breeds can be prone to deafness, like the boxers, Old English sheepdogs, Jack Russell terriers, and many more.

http://www.lethalwhites.com/

I have personally met a lot of dogs that are deaf, and many who have impaired vision. The owners aren't aware of it, and neither is their vet. Every time I approach someone about their dog, they always proclaim that what I'm seeing can't be true, because the dog was just examined by their vet. It is true! The number of deaf and visually impaired dogs is on the rise. You can thank puppy mills and careless breeders for this.

While I hate to break the news to these unsuspecting dog owners and dog lovers - and part of me believes they would live a great life not knowing about their dog's disability - I know it's not really a disability! I also feel it's important to prevent the dog from being punished for something he has no control over. If a dog is called, and does not come, the owner may get frustrated if he doesn't know that his dog is deaf.

I try to break the news gently and deliver it with an incredibly positive tone, but the look on their faces is heartbreaking when they start to believe me and realize that their dog is deaf.

As this revelation sinks in, I also see the anger on their faces as they think about the breeder, the price they paid for the dog, and the disappointment in their veterinarian who missed it. It does make you wonder, doesn't it?

Regarding the Aussie I mentioned earlier from Polk County Animal Services, we did rescue him. We named him Anderson Cooper and he is available for adoption!

Jen Wilson with Anderson Cooper

Dedication

This book is dedicated to all of the dogs that taught me so much, never knowing that I knew so very little.

Winter

About the Dog Liberator

The Dog Liberator is a small foster-driven non-profit dog rescue located in Central Florida. Founded by Gisele Veilleux in 2009, they have continued to rescue approximately 200 dogs per year, over 700 to date.

The Dog Liberator focuses on rescuing dogs in danger, thus preventing highly adoptable dogs from being destroyed.

While their primary focus is rescue, they also provide education to the general public regarding a wide range of topics, including adopting senior dogs, adopting deaf and/or blind dogs, the importance of spaying/neutering, training, behavior, and diet.

Visit the Dog Liberator's website for more information. http://thedogliberator.com or find them on Facebook, http://www.Facebook.com/dogliberator

Other Books about The Dog Liberator

All of the books written about The Dog Liberator are true stories, written in real-time.

<u>Bartholomew's Fight to Survive</u>

Published January 2013

http://www.lulu.com/spotlight/giseleveilleux

I'm Your Huckleberry

Published December, 2012

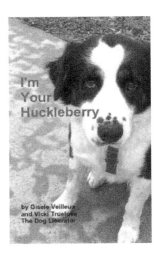

http://www.lulu.com/shop/gisele-veilleux/im-your-huckleberry/paperback/product-20620093.html

The Story of Penelope, a Puppy Mill Dog,

Originally published in 2008

and revised in 2012.

http://www.lulu.com/shop/gisele-veilleux/the-story-of-penelope/paperback/product-20433861.html

All of Gisele Veilleux's published work can be found on

http://www.lulu.com/spotlight/giseleveilleux

Made in the USA
Coppell, TX
29 January 2020